True Friendship
Within
The Youth of
America

Eric Martin

Additional copies of this book may be obtained by writting :
E.W.M Enterprise inc
p.o.box 153108
Dallas,tx 75315
e-mail- ewmenterpriseinc@mail.com
e-mail- ericmartin@mail.com
website www.ewmenterpriseinc.webs.com

ISBN:978-0-578-08160

Acknowledgements

I WOULD LIKE TO ANALOGUE THOSE'S WHO HELP ME IN MY LIFE TO BECOME THE PERSON I AM TODAY THAT IS NOT HEAR TO SEE THIS WONDERFUL TRANSFORMATION TAKE PLACE!

PAPA ROSEY, RJ-BIG MAMA, OLA-BIG MAMA, BIG RUBE-BIG DADDY, RUBIN-EL-RUB-O, AUNT SHEERLY, MR & MRS. COOPER, AUNT BELV, UNCLE CHARLES, UNCLE RAY, GARLAND HARRIS AND WHO-DAT ?

D.D.
LIL CUZ DE MARCUS

OF COURSE THEIRS MORE IF I LEFT SOME ONE OUT PLACE THE NAME

HERE --

FOR THOSE STILL ALIVE I MAY HAVE USED YOUR NAME IN MY BOOK ONLY TO SHOW HOW YOU ARE DEEPLY APPRECIATED
NOTHING MORE! TO ALL MY FRIENDS FAMILY TEACHERS THAT PUT UP WITH ME I LOVE YOU ALL! OF COURSE MY WIFE DANA MARTIN WHO SUPPORTED ME IN GETTING THIS BOOK DONE LAST BUT NOT LESS MY TWO KIDS ERIC JR. & ERIC'KA

ANY ONE LEFT OUT PUT YOUR NAME

HERE --

TABLE OF CONTENTS

Chapter 5

THE GIFTS OF HAVING A FRIEND

Chapter 6

DETECTING THE FRIEND OR ENEMY

Chapter 7

THE POSITIVE OPPORTUNITIES OF FRIENDSHIP

Part 37: A Friend Who Receives Promotions and Second Chances.

Part 38: A Friend Achieving Goals-Help From The Community

Part 39: Partaking in Favorable Circumstances with a Friend

Part 40: The Value of Keeping a Promise to a Friend Promise

Part 41: Seeing the Importance of Motivation and Success

Chapter 8

SEEING THE VALUE IN CULTIVATING POTENTIAL

Part 42: Not Allowing a Friend to Waste Their Talent

Part 43: Knowing the Importance of Being Goal-Oriented

Part 44: The Possibility Thinking Friend

Part 45: Enjoying the Go-Getter Friend

Part 46: The Friend Being a Positive Force in a Competitive World

PREFACE

First of all, this book "True Friendship within the Youth of America", is an inspiring self-help and self-motivating book with material containing excellent principles for success. The reader can use it as a guiding tool. You must understand that True Friendship" is a valuable commodity that carries more weight than material gains. Have an open mind and be flexible in the message that is being given to you throughout the concrete contents of this book. Each of the eight chapters outlined will help you understand the positive of true friendship, which you can utilize in your life to better yourself and enrich your relationship, with your friends, and on the other hand, the negatives, that will help you to avoid these traits that trifle friendships.

Chapters One and Two simply give you basic characteristics that you may possess in terms of "Friends" who can be an asset to one another or a hindrance towards the success of a friendship.

Chapter Three and Four consists of the betrayal factor in a friendship and a friends' word, as this can mean a lot in terms of the friendship having elasticity. It also deals with the warning signs to be aware of, what is necessary when trying to build enormous trust and how this is effectively practiced.

Chapter Five is the heart and soul of the book that pertains to being grateful and appreciative of the "Gift" a friend possesses.

Chapter Six and Seven contents pertain to knowing when you are in the company of a good or bad friend. The positive opportunities behind a friend will open many doors for you to expand your horizon and help you in making wise when engaging in activities with friends.

Finally, Chapter Eight is the icing on the cake, recognizing the need for cultivating your potential, but not allowing negativity or waste. Nor, becoming dormant in your growth and development to become a success, either for you or to others, in regards to the future generations.

E.W.M. ENTERPRISE INC. PRESENTS…..

In this book, I mainly focused on the "at-risk" youth, whom everyone has given up on, as well as the youth whose voice needs to be heard. I hope that their journey through reading this book will be fulfilled in-keeping with the original intent of this book.

Chapter 1

What Is a Friend?

Part 1: A Loyalist
Someone who is faithful to a person.

I am sure if not all of us, one way or another, are seeking faith in someone we can lean heavily on, an individual we can count on to take care of business for us in our time of need. Young people today are missing an important ingredient with regard to feelings of devoted affection. You can lean your shoulders on a loyalist with no feelings of regret. He will be the glue to keep a classmate, teammate, or playmate together. These relationships will always have a person who is unfaithful and, therefore you must be careful in classifying an individual you would consider as a "Friend".

Example #1: If Erin chose to have Walter hold something valuable for him and trust Walter to take care of it until he come back for it, than Erin must make sure that Walter is loyal in his actions to do what is right, or Erin will be at fault for exercising bad wisdom in selecting Walter to be a loyal friend. A loyalist has responsibilities that he does not take light because he does not want to hold a bad reputation, nor does he want people to look down on him. A loyalist firmly believes if given the opportunity to become a leader, he accepts the burdens knowing everybody will be deeply affected by decisions and actions. If a loyalist plans are not carried out effectively, than he realizes that damages cannot be corrected for all concerned including him. He is careful to be patient and diligent in making a move leaving no room for error.

Example #2: A leader such as Erin, President of Point Blank Entertainment is a friend who is loyal and deeply holds common beliefs, views and ideas that are firm in his allegiance to the board members within the company. Otherwise, someone else must be placed in that position to uphold its credibility. A loyal friend wants people to rely on him having the qualifications to get the job done. A loyalist such as Erin wants to be able to stay upon completion of each project, "Mission complete."

Part 2: A Congenial Person
Someone having the same taste, habits, or temperament.

I know that congeniality such as common habits and tastes are important when it comes to "True Friendship." A congenial person does not choose to block opportunities for their friend when they choose to be successful. They fittingly suit their friends' interest, and having fun plays a big part in whatever they do together. A congenial person is easy to get along with and possess high social skills necessary when in the midst of people from all lifestyles. You do not want to cross a congenial person the wrong way. A congenial friend who possess a quality such as: kindness that a friend feels comfortable being around. A congenial person has a friendly disposition and is sincere in the way they carries themselves around their friends.

 Example #1: If Brian goes to the recreation center to play basketball with Damon, they will have fun as well as teach each other various basketball techniques, they will also enhance each other to become better basketball players. If Brian suffers an injury while playing basketball, Damon is willing to help find the proper medical attention to help Brian. When you are at your lowest point, a congenial person will be the one to help you.

Example #2: While Britney is going through a trial such as failing in school, which could cause her to drop out. Her friend Andra'Nae is there to provide support for Britney by helping her to have confidence to perform well in school. Andra'Nae wants to create a positive social atmosphere where ideas flow and solutions to problems are easier to come by. Andra'Nae is the type of person who has Britney's best interest at heart and is willing to tutor her to improve her grades, protect her from students who want to degrade or make a mockery out her concerning the grades she have been making. Andra'Nae is always courteous and warm-hearted around Britney's parents, classmates, and school officials. She is a positive influence to all those in her presence and always walks around the school campus with a smile and an upbeat attitude.

Part 3: A Comforter
Someone who soothes in time of grief or fear.

Young people today should display comforting qualities towards friends, which are necessary in times of loss, damages, and failures. Usually when a young person is down, he looks for role models such as coaches, parents, ministers, mentors, or counselors to life them up with the positive tools that they posses. However, in friendships, a young person must exercise the capacity to give physical and spiritual ease, which a "Comforter" possesses. His desire to help his friend can prevent him form entering a downward cycle into negative activities, which will result in his downfall. When his friend is being ridiculed and made a mockery of by people, then a comforter soothes him by giving encouraging words to keep his mind off the negativity.

For instance, if Alyssa is fired from her job, she may decide to go horseback riding with Kamora to help relieve stress after receiving the bad news. Sure, Alyssa will go through periods of frustration and distress, but horseback riding will relieve the tension from her setback. During this activity, Kamora will share with Alyssa some positive things about horseback riding while checking out the beautiful scenery overlooking the mountains.

A comforter understands a friend might not be strong enough to handle rejection and denial, so he must boost the confidence level of his friend to the point where he can withstand the storm. He bears his friends burdens and says, "Put it all on me" or "Let me take you by the hand and carry you," while not wanting a favor in return. A comforter utilizes his tools to make a friend feel better about their selves. He understands his services are important to the world and does beyond just consoling this friend. He is the type of person that does not mind doing work that is being of service that requires helping people with insufficient needs. He has experienced the darker side of life at a one time, but wants his friend to only meditate on peaceful things. Young people may learn the right road to success is going through trial and error that can make them stronger in life.

Part 4: A Supporter
Someone maintaining a position so as to keep from falling or slipping.

I chose this topic for young people because they posse's dreams and ideas that they want to bring into fruition and the help of a support group or support system is necessary for them to believe that they are possible. I believe that they are possible. I believe a friend can do well from the benefits of a one on one support system. This is where a supporter comes in to provide strong moral, physical, and mental support for his friend who might need this help immediately. Remember people in society do render a service of this nature charging a fee, but a supporter just wants his friend to receive the necessary help he needs to achieve his goals. I believe many young people give up to soon in life because of the lack of support, which was not enough to give them the push to reach the top.

For example, a common subject that many young people experience a lot is "obesity." A friend such as Andrea would help Beverly by including a rigid exercise program, a healthy diet, and proper rest. Andrea will encourage and motivate Beverly to produce wonderful results. The main thing Andrea is concerned about is Beverly's appearance out in society whether she is shopping at the mall, at a public gathering, or the negative treatment she may receive from people in society.

Andrea is a friend who utilizes her role as a supporter to help Beverly mediate on healthy thoughts throughout the course of the day. She knows her support will make a difference in Beverly experiencing a brand new life.

Young people can teach adults the importance of supporting one another when negative elements like greed, jealousy, and selfishness are exhibited. These habits must be broken at an early age for their poison has destroyed many people's lives. A supporter is humbly willing to accept lesser roles with his friend in charge. He does not want the credit for everything but is always willing to give a helping hand. He cares about the growth and protection of his friend's status. Once friends learn to implement support for one another, it will be easy for them to work together.

Part 5: An Acquaintance
Someone possessing the knowledge and information.

This topic will help young people to avoid pitfalls before they decide to enter a "Friendship." The reason young people should establish knowing someone first in a friendship is because it will make them familiar with who they are dealing with and it will be easier for them to make an honest assessment that this friendship will work out. An acquaintance is a good friend who wants his friend who wants his friend to make careful choices and be aware of his surrounding because they play a key part in his success. This individual understanding that his friend is similar to someone needing a map with the information giving him the right route to take. There is a saying, "What you don't know can't hurt you," but an acquaintance wants to inform and familiarize his friend of any danger that might lurk in his company.

For instance, Maurice is excited about taking Demarcus to a "Science Fair." Maurice already knows that the information and experience Demarcus absorbs from this event is valuable to him because he will obtain excellent knowledge on volcanoes and geography and will learn how to analyze volcanic ashes. First, Maurice recognizes the interest and desire that Demarcus has for volcanoes as well geography. While at the booth of the science fair, Maurice introduces Demarcus to certified specialists who are trained and heavily experienced in these fields, which can give Demarcus a head start over the young people who desire to pursue careers in the same fields. Demarcus appreciates Maurice helping him to know more about volcanoes and geography.

Many times young people while in the midst of all kinds of negativity, an acquaintance can help them stay on the right course. Remember, "True Friendship," embodies closeness and young people must exercise good wisdom to achieve this. With the youth being our future, we must be on guard for adults who would keep them from not knowing what is best for them. An acquaintance as a close friend looks at the bigger perspective with regard to his friend's current and future success and wants him to know anything that will upgrade his position.

Part 6: A Convivialist
Someone who is fond of feasting, harmonious surrounds and good company.

I am inspired to include this topic of a convivialist person with regard to "True Friendship" because it is healthy and positive when friends get together. It is so many negative activities in our society, which young people are influenced by and it could lead them into disarray. Conviviality governs precise decisions for his friends throughout a social gathering. He knows the right company for his friend to be around. Young people are wise to refrain from joining gangs, going to parties for pleasurable purposes, and going to negative places. A convivialist chooses the word healthy in terms of gatherings for his friend because he wants him to be aware of the type, quality, and temperament being exemplified in the get-together. A convivialist knows that teamwork, high self-esteem and good morals can be developed when his friend is around his company.

For instance, Latasha has scheduled an event such as going to the history of art museum with Camille. Latasha hopes Camille gets more out of it than just the actual attendance of this event. She wants Camille to grow from the study, preservation, exhibition of works of artistic and historical value. Going to the museum is a tremendous education experience for Camille while at the same time she's learning about other cultures and expanding her horizons. Camille appreciates Latasha giving her this experience, the knowledge of something different and unique. Latasha would love to do this again in the future if the opportunity presents itself again. First, a convivialist encourages the right motives and intentions when going to concert or parties with his friend because he knows not all of the participants are there for the right reason. Many young people neglect concerns for a positive structure when it comes to the choices they make while attending public gatherings. Many people look to far ahead while wasting precious and valuable time believing they can make up what they took for granted. He helps his friend to learn to adjust, to have patience, and being forthright while in the midst of good company. Remember, he gravitates to organizing positive events for his friends with the intent to give him a more positive outlook on life.

Part 7: An Alliance Person
Someone who unionizes.

I choose this topic for the youth of America because of the powerful significance in the word "Unity." An alliance person joins his friend in a mutual interest for their benefit. Once he and his friend are on the same page, the sharing, helping, and teaching one another will become natural to them. He is firmly behind and an enforcer of saying, "United we stand and divided we fall" to his friend. An alliance person loves to join with his friend in any activity looking to advance their dreams together. He is enthusiastic on being the one who organizes, plans, and arranges the interest his friend has. Young people usually look at alliance as coming from a leadership mode and true enough it is, but all that is necessary is the desire to share your success with someone else other than yourself.

An alliance person teaches his friends valuable lessons hoping their other friendships, which might be on rocky terms, learn to utilize the tools he possess helping them in their situations. Whereas a narrow-minded young person would have an idea to start a school, hospital, or newspaper route business, a broad-minded young person with a bigger vision in a united fashion sees the potential for greater lives being saved, more people being educated, and a larger newspaper business delivering information to people knowing what's going on around the world.

Chapter 2

"WHO IS NOT A FRIEND"

Part 8: A Hostile Person
Someone feeling or displaying enmity or antagonism.

A hostile person exhibits destructive forces that oppose any good thing his friend does. He is considered an adversary who does not want his friend to succeed in any positive endeavors. He does not exercise hospitable qualities toward his friend nor does he have his friend's best interest at heart. A hostile person does not exercise self-control and will lash out at any minute or time. It is hard for a friend to hang around or be in his company. Anger is the root to a hostile person's make-up and if not contained or channeled correctly it will lead to a catastrophic ending. He is negative and disrespectful to his friend and loves to cause violence.

This individual thrives on tearing his friend down whether by words or actions whenever his friend receives praise and honor form teachers, coaches, or mentors. He is against teamwork and for conflict and tension being the main poison in a friendship. Harmony cannot be achieved among friends as long as contention and malice is present. Hostility comes in all forms from just a simple opposition where friends are not agreeing on a common subject to acts of animosity where violent acts are present. The youth today must avoid these situations to be successful. Being fair among friends in a competitive event is a beautiful thing to practice, but when hostility is present then hurt and pain will be the outcome.

Unless a hostile person eradicates the poison of hostility from his personality the "True Friendship" can never be achieved. Hostility is the main reason many young people lives have been shattered at an early age. For a young person's life to be constructive, he must rid himself of this cancerous seed. When young people choose to engaged in activities such as roller-skating, going to the amusement part, and playing video games etc, which bring out healthy values in young lives.

Part 9: A Bad Prospect
Someone examining and bringing to the scent negative possibilities.

The primary purpose of this topic as well as other topics within this chapter is to enlighten our youth on the dangers of what is not a friend so that they can form healthy friendly friendships and become successful in life. A bad prospect shows his friend that he cannot be trusted and engaging in negativity is a common practice. He does not see anything wrong in showing his friend negative acts, knowing this will not build friends up but tear them down. You will always find him with the wrong crowds exercising bad practice in these settings as well. Knowing whatever his intentions are will be detrimental to his friend, a Bad prospect proceeds anyway to put his friend in a wreck.

He is the type of person that gives false information about his credentials to his friend to give himself a better position than his friend and others as well. Instead of exercising honesty and fairness, a bad prospect rather use this false information toward his advantage when engaging in activities with a friend. He does not fit the criteria of a true "Role Model" because he wants to show the negative quality instead of positive steps toward reaching a goal. As long as young people are driven toward choices and thoughts must be channeled in the right direction before we can rise above bad prospect or acts that are not beneficial to us.

For instance, an election at a high school was coming up to run for student body president and Jamel had given the principal his portfolio to show his credentials qualifying him for the position. Terence, his closest friend had selected Jamel and had vigorously put together a strong campaign to get him elected. Terence did not know that Jamel had falsified his documents in the portfolio trying to take the easy route to be elected as student body president. Jamel was a bad prospect believing he could get away with this deception towards the students who would vote and the school officials at the high school. Eventually, Jamel was expelled from the school and everyone at the school including community members was devastated about his actions.

Part 10: Unfavorable Person
Someone who is negative and not desiring what is embodied.

Everyday young people are introduced to activities that are disapproved, discomforting, or dishonored in our society. An unfavorable person does not believe in being equal with his friend even if they have the same goals in mind. This individual could have an excellent plan that will work out for both him and his friend, but he still will not be supportive of its overall success. He puts up this wall disunity between himself and his friend so that harmony and peace cannot be embodied in their friendship. Negativity rule in his arena to the point he is willing to give out as well as receive unfavorable opinions. Young people need to avoid the bad seeds; this individual spreads which is not healthy to them. An unfavorable person's negative agenda can only lead to further acts of corruption which can cause him to end up in a whole lot of trouble. He is against giving something to his friend as a token of love, affection, or remembrance because his heart is not in the right place and he is not well intentioned. Many young people have the ability to formulate ideas for the cause of something good, but an unfavorable person will not support this matter. He likes to have the advantage over his friend when it comes to solutions to everyday problems. Young people must not exercise this negative act because they will never develop the attitude that treating people with good care is the right thing and healthy.

Our society has a long way to go when we promote illicit language produce illicit clothes, and allow non-mentoring material to be the focal point of our young people's lives. Anybody with good morals, principles, and ethics about themselves would disfavor these practices but if we continue to allow this to occur, it shows us our youth will never receive the proper guidance they need to refrain from them. Many of our young people have good intention and have a listening ear to what is beneficial for them.

Part 11: A Person Not Having Your Best Interest at Heart
Someone not in you corner or looks forward to your setbacks and downfalls.

There are activities or affairs that a person with a bad interest shares is never beneficial to his friend. The key to success in a "True Friendship" falls within someone being in your corner and having your best interest at heart, a person with bad interest does not fit theses criteria. The negative act this individual conducts only draws a friend from the right path which shows he enjoys contributing to his friend's demise. His original intent was to cause financial, physical, or mental damages to a friend's status while elevating his own. He is truly not your friend because he earnestly wishes your downfall. He will even start an organization to where his original intent is to cause a setback for his so clamed friend thinking he is helping him by joining the organization.

Young people are wiser these days when associating with a friend possessing bad interest qualities because they know that common goals cannot be reach together. This individual has negative qualities which can catch his friend off guard meaning his friend has to be aware of this. It is sad to see young people engaging in non positive activities on a daily basis who will regress instead of progress in their endeavors once associated with his type of individual. Many people who are introduced to things harmful to them must learn to search or grab hold of positive influences to keep from entering into disarray. The reason boys and girls clubs, YMCA's and youth positive workshops are set up in our communities is to teach young kids about the value of teamwork, self=discipline, and to equip them will well-rounded life principles. Once a young person exercises bad interest in these affairs within these groups, then the common purpose of which each group represents is ruined. A young person who wants something out of life and likes to enjoy the company of good friends must be careful to find someone who encourages his success and holds deeply his best interest at heart.

Part 12: An Agitator
Someone who stirs up and upsets emotionally a cause.

This topic will help young people gain a better understanding to refrain from being an agitator especially when it comes to "True Friendship." An agitator loves to shake up the normal flow of things by stirring up confusing creating tension with people they consider friends. An agitator is so caught up in creating disorder in the friendship and is never willing to admit the fact that he is doing anything wrong. When a friend is focused on peaceful thoughts and actions, an agitator would cause a negative atmosphere. He thrives on instigating rumors, lies, and negative stories while tarnishing his friend's reputation and bringing him down.

For example: When Shawn is performing outstanding in school showing scholastic promise, then Deandre stirs up false rumors around campus trying to cause Shawn's downfall. It is a shame to see Deandre behave like this knowing that Shawn takes pride in his education only to have Deandre wanting him to fail. Young people need an education to help further their goals in life but the role that Deandre plays as an agitator in this situation is not helpful to any young person aspiring to further their education.

Young people who carry bad motives and intentions around their friends who have good hearts should try to get rid of agitated behaviors they possess so that they can have an open channel for peace and harmony again. "True Friendship" cannot be established with a person taking on an agitator's role. A sharp person recognizes the body language and demeanor of this individual. Our youth in society these days have enough common sense to know the dangers which could happen in their foreseeable future if they choose to hang around an agitator. If young people whish to continue in the right path then eliminate this negative trait as an agitator form their life.

Part 13: Jealous Person
Someone resentful or bitter of being replaced by a rival to another's affection.

Many of our youth, one time or another will experience the jealous disposition of someone with regards to their success. There is always someone in society who does not want to see you be successful in life, nor to help someone else become successful. This individual is fearful that his friend will be given a greater status then himself which he felt at first he should have been placed in that position. Another root of jealousy is bitterness which can tear up a young person's soul and appearance. There should be no room for jealousy when every young person is unique in their talent in where he can excel to be an asset to society. Jealously is a cancer to our young people growth and it hinders them from being successful. Even when young people work hard to achieve a goal and give it their best shot and their friend's in the same field achieve a higher notoriety, they must be content and not allow jealousy to bring about division in the friendship.

Sometimes young people are jealous of their friend's idea, property, or associates when they have their own free choices to select from. A jealous person does not have enough sense to realize there is plenty in the world for everybody to have, share, or give away. A lot of hurt and pain can result from jealousy if it is not dealt with properly. Once a jealous person removes this from his personality, he will see many doors open to him and most of all his friends will enjoy being around him and doing activities together. Being jealous of each other is a waste of time to people when they can be cultivating their skills to shape and mold each other's future. A young person who wants to make a difference in our society does not want to get in the way of another persons success but plants seeds of growth and upward mobility. Young people must learn to be driven by their dreams and goals and not allow the negative force of jealousy to set precedence on their friendships.

Part 14: A Malicious Person
Someone desiring to harm others or to see others suffer.

Many young people need to be aware of the dangers behind the acts of a malicious person so that they can stay on the right path in life. Many communities and especially inner city communities are flooded with young innocent people being victims of malicious acts leading to death. One of the seeds that malice is derived from is hatred, which in itself is a destructive quality. Young people do malicious acts to others for fear of the unknown, therefore triggering them to hate without a reason. Even though an individual does nothing to have a malicious person act like this towards him, it does not stop him form going forward with his negativity. It should be easy, to tell our young people why are hospitals, confinement centers, and cemeteries are full of young innocent lives that did not deserve this treatment from this type of individual. The only thing on a malicious person's mind is to see his friends worse off than he was instead of exercising good principles and ethics to wish him the best. Also, this goes along with doing something out of spite to a friend to hurt him or her. Committing such a horrible act is the primary reason why a lot of dreams, ideas, and visions are cut short of being fulfilled because a malicious person chooses to inflict harm on a person with the potential to be somebody grates in life. Many people from all walks of life are guilty of this.

The best tool or remedy to rid a person from conducting malicious acts is to demonstrate actions of unconditional love towards this person, learning to accept him despite his shortcomings, and not letting him bear himself up constantly over his failures. Also, let him now that to harm people will not make him a better person, but to have more enemies in his life. Being this type of person is not good people can be their own worse enemy, but learning to finish positive and strong in their endeavors will help them upon entering adulthood and cherishing precious years ahead of them.

Chapter 3

What are the Consequences of Betraying a Friend?

Part 15: The Price of Deceiving a Friend
Someone causing a friend to believe what is not true.

Many young people are caught in the trap of deception from their friends needing to be aware of its hazards. Once Dean deceives Travis he shows he cannot be trusted. Dean feels this will give him the advantage over Travis, not knowing at the end this deceptive act will come back to haunt him. A person who utilizes deceptive acts on a friend feels this is necessary to uphold and elevate his reputation. Dean portrays this good guy image in front of Travis thinking that he will not know about this, but all along Travis is aware of this art of trickery. Dean does not care about using Travis as a pawn to further his agenda.

This is a new day for our young people when if our goal is to have "True Friendship" without the art of deception. A wise young person knows that bad karma will result from committing deceptive acts towards a friend. You pay a terrible price when you mislead people into doing things they ordinarily would not do. Dean is a shiest person who likes to hoodwink and therefore Travis should recognize that Dean is not in his corner. Dean needs to remove this cancerous quality from his make-up and by making this conscientious decision many channels of success will be open to him.

Young people can only scale the heights of success once they cleanse themselves from the filth of deception. Young people must learn to be careful how they treat their friends and make an effort to refrain from deceit acts, which could hinder them from becoming successful. It is a travesty for Dean to use the art of deception on Travis when it comes to establishing true friendship. I encourage the youth to try to exercise sincerity in a friendship and watch the amazing results of bonding and closeness.

Part 16: A Traitor Who Wants to Win at All Costs

Someone willfully betraying a cause or trust without concerns of a friend.

Young people should avoid the traits that a traitor possesses in selling out their friends', family and community for selfish gains. A traitor will do this all the time for something better not caring about the best interest of the next person. He is simply someone who is supposed to be on the same team as you but decides to jump ship and go to another team. Therefore, his loyalty was not there to begin with; otherwise he would have stayed where he was. A traitor will decide to do something else being influenced either by the art of manipulation or just feeling more comfortable around other people or groups. In our society, a traitor's actions are unacceptable and I am begging all young people to not follow this example. This shows your true character when you go against people who do not mind looking out for you or who show loyalty towards you.

The loyalty factor is thrown out the window when dealing with this type of individual. How can a friend conduct serious business with each other when the evidence of trust is not present? It is a good thing for young people to receive positive advice on the harmful qualities a traitorous person possess from someone, which can prevent them from making decisions that are detrimental to their goals in life.

For example: Melvin is on a football team but decides he wants to join Eric's team because Melvin will be given more playing time and he feels more compatible with the players on Eric's team. Now, the league director, Melvin's coach and his teammates calls him a "traitor" and now they look at Melvin in an untrustworthy way. The fact that Melvin was comfortable with his decision should not disrupt friendship, but inadvertently it did. Therefore, when young people decide to go in another direction whether it's with a team, group or cause then it could easily start to form enemies instead of friends. It is not healthy to disown your friend by becoming a traitor because "True Friendship" is about demonstrating faithfulness towards each other and staying together through it all thick and then.

Part 17: The Outcome of Tarnishing a Friends Reputation

Someone who diminishes or taints a specific characteristic of something.

This is a degrading thing to do to a friend and young people must be cognizant of the danger tarnishing a friend's reputation can cause. First, Deandre must ask himself, if it is worth it to bring Charles down knowing he many need his support down the road. To go out of your way to hurt someone is a cruel and mean thing to do even if you harbor ill feelings toward this person. In the society we live in these days, a court of law will decide if someone is being tarnished as a victim by someone targeting him to cause injury or harm. The truth of the matter is close friends can iron out their negative qualities in a cordially manner without outside help because a mutual understanding will be arrived between these two.

Deandre should try to do his best in maintaining a high standard of achievement and not be wrapped in the competitive aspect concerning Charles achievement. Once, Deandre learns to stay focused on his own goals then trying to hurt Charles will not enter his arena. You cannot replace anything sentimental but Deandre takes pride in spoiling Charles personal property. This is a terrible thing to see young people go out of their way to perform tarnishing acts on each other only to curtail the fact that working together to achieve a common goal is a wonderful thing. Young people must learn to be driven with helping each other and motivate them more than trying to tarnish each other through fraudulent means. When you surround yourself around positive people, it propels you to do positive things that block out negativity such as tarnishing a friend's reputation.

Part 18: Taking Advantage of Friends Generosity
Someone who is not noble and forbearing in thought or behavior.

Young people should not breach the contract of generosity with their friends because they should be aware of the betrayal when taking advantage of them. Lisa is ruthless to the point she refuses to produce an income in order to support her. She relies on Keisha for handouts all of the time. She is definitely one who shows no consideration for the next person. Lisa looks at Keisha's generosity as her weakness and wishes to use her in a way which is selfish on her part.

Keisha might not exercise wisdom in giving, to the point whereas her abundance is being misused. She doesn't care who reaps the benefits but little does she know crafty people such as Lisa lurk around to prey on her. A lot of times we give so much, not knowing people with bad intentions such as Lisa. She gets a thrill out taking advantage of Keisha's generosity and plots and schemes with a different agenda, which is not in Keisha's best interest. Lisa definitely needs to learn the hard way. This would teach her a valuable lesson on conducting negative acts. On the other hand, Keisha must recognize that she is being taken advantage of and would be better off breaking off the association with Lisa and associating herself with someone who appreciates her generosity. A lot of young people come from strong upbringings from parents who instill in them good moral values and principles. Fortunately, this prevents them from conducting such negative acts.

Lisa, who chooses to takes advantage of Keisha's generosity, looks forward to excuses to justify why she can use Keisha, which isn't right. Keisha never shows rebellious or selfishness towards Lisa. She knows that she needs help, but Lisa must also make an effort to help herself as well. There's an old saying "help those who help themselves." There are always situations in which young people tend to get in trouble, resulting in them seeking help from others. When this situation arises, one should be considerate and careful not to take advantage of a friend's generosity in helping and assisting them.

Part 19: The Results of Destroying a Friend
Someone who ruins completely and renders destruction all they touch.

Of course, our youth must exercise wisdom when they have nothing to do other than trying to destroy a friend for whatever reason this may be.

Donna, who detects this, must get out of a friendship for her own safety and well being. Our youth should include in their agenda, the desire to see their friends be in good spirit and health. Unfortunately, due to the lack of direction or purse in a young person's life, this becomes an obstacle. A lot of mistakes are made in our lives and they are due to negative influences. These negative influences tend to lead us to destructive behaviors and doing terrible things to each other.

Samantha doesn't recognize the pain and hurt she cause Donna's parents, teachers and peers when she continuously tries to tear down and crash Donna's dreams, goals and aspirations. This is disruptive to Donna, who is trying to stay focused and goal-oriented, avoiding Samantha's efforts to tear her down. It takes hard work, dedication and motivation to rise above the hurdles, obstacles and life-challenges that young people have to face.

E.W. Martin

For example, one of the things Donna must be careful about is Samantha's destructive behavior, offering her drugs and alcohol. She has to be strong and smart enough to know this is very addictive and harmful to her health and well being. If, Donna brings on this form of destruction, even though in her thinking, she believes this as a form of relaxation, a way of taking their mind off their problems and not knowing this will only lead to more problems. Addiction leads to change in appearance, personality and decreases motivation to achieve ones goals. Once the wrong choice has been made to partake of these mind-altering chemicals, it would be wise to rectify the situation by seeking help to quit and enjoy the road to sobriety. It doesn't matter if the outcome isn't as serious as violence or abuse, it is still negative.

Samantha is like a loose cannon ready to explode at any time. She resists the guidance from a counselor, mentor or role model, people trying to help her get a grip on herself. Samantha does not set a good example for her peers.

Chapter 4

"ALL A FRIEND HAS IS HIS WORD"

Part 20: The Benefit of Being a Quiet Friend
Someone silent, marked by tranquility and peacefulness.

This topic has very important benefits when it comes to quietness. The youth can hear and be more in-tune with themselves' better. Barbara, who exercises silence, has the advantage over Charlotte, because she is more in-tune with positive signals, such as confidence, happiness and peace. Barbara can enjoy tranquil acts like mediation and prayer, which helps in a spiritual aspect. Many people believe quiet people are more studious than others when it comes to being educated. The truth of the matter is Barbara only speaks when spoken to or when she has something worthwhile to talk about. There is a true proverb or saying "A fool is thought to be wise when he says nothing at all." To put it in short context, to be a quiet friend like Barbara has benefits such as serenity, which includes freedom from agitation, anger and strife.

Barbara knows strength is derived from being quiet, because the less people know about you the better you are. Barbara is not showy or boastful in her demeanor around Charlotte. She merely conducts her business quietly and effectively, getting strong reactions from other people. Another positive trait derived from Barbara is harmony in the midst of turbulence and turmoil. Sure enough, it is not easy to always exercise quietness when things around you are spiraling out of control, but this method is the best when trying to out chaos. Barbara will have Charlotte and people in general willing to do basic things together; harmoniously playing video games, going to the amusement parks, dining out, going to the movies and other activities and events in a peaceful manner. These are activities Barbara enjoys. She wants to make things fun for Charlotte and herself. Making the most of a good time is important to Barbara.

I commend any young person who seeks this quality in a friend. They will be admired by the masses who love soothing dispositions. Solitude can be a perfect example of quietness. You can choose to have Barbara as a partner and not have to worry about any negative feedback from her or creating any negativity. Young people, if you will try the quiet disposition when you are with you friends. You will experience growth in mutual respect and understanding for each other.

Part 21: The Dangers of a Talkative Person
Sometimes talking can be hazardous

Young people need to adhere to a positive word of advice or encouragement, which helps them scale to heights to reach their goals. On the other hand be on guard or watchful of a talkative friend. There is nothing wrong with talking and holding conversations as long as it is constructive or holds substance to a topic. One of the most prevalent dangers of Rhonda is spreading rumors and gossip. In this case, Rhonda should hold her peace because she can cause problems for the people implicated in the rumors of whom she is gossiping about. Another hazard of Rhonda is using words for persuasion or bad influence to be little another.

Usually Rhonda is chatty to the point whereas she enjoys the attention and crowds, which in the long run does more harm than good. Common courtesy and respect are not traits which Rhonda does not possess nor can she give a good example to someone else about this. Rhonda can be an articulate speaker to or for Leslie, but all of this can go out the door if she is not speaking with substance or eloquence. Rhonda cannot hold a secret which Leslie would advise her to keep her mouth closed about. Rhonda can cause Leslie to be tired of her mainly for her talkative ways. This trait must be avoided for "True Friendship" to be established. When friends are discreet and treat each other cordially than they can have a durable and lasting relationship.

For example: Rhonda goes out with Leslie to a positive event where many other young people are gathered to learn, share, and enjoy various types of video games and the new technology with regard to future business in video games and their amusement. Leslie came to get educated and have a little fun. Now while at a particular booth of the amusement park, an instructor was giving valuable knowledge on a new product, but Rhonda rudely interrupted talking over others who where trying to listen and learn new points in the video game field. The bottom line is refrain form being a talkative person such as Rhonda because few words with meaning are more valuable than a host of words that are trivial.

Part 22: The Rewards a Friend Reaps from an Encouraging Word
Someone who inspires with hope, courage and confidence.

First, in a friendship setting the fruits of an encouraging word will automatically cheer up someone needing to be uplifted. To hear something which provides a boost to Stephanie will give more motivation and incentive for her to reach a goal. The magnitude behind an encouraging word is like supporting or aiding a matter which was not strong to begin with. If Stephanie needs an encouraging word and Cynthia provides hope for her in a gloomy situation, than Cynthia will receive blessings and good things will happen for Cynthia. Anytime we give spark to someone shedding light for them, we should be happy knowing our own status will be elevated. Sometimes Cynthia can give more help to Stephanie by an uplifting word than by her actions, showing Stephanie to keep her head up and remain faithful. Everyday, young people are going through trials and tribulations. An encouraging word can make the difference between Stephanie going forward with confidence in what she is trying to achieve and giving up. A true saying is, "A winner never quits and a quitter never wins." The more we help each other with words of encouragement, the more achievers we will have. The youth are assets to our society.

The rewards Stephanie reaps from an encouraging word does not necessarily have to be in a material sense, just as longs as it helps Stephanie advance and better her current position. As long as Stephanie has made progress and the positive word she received was the right type at the time, then Stephanie feels content which she may not realize it is a reward. A lot of times, Cynthia's duty to Stephanie is to help in any way she can without expecting anything in return, but Cynthia may forget and deviate from what is supposed to be held dear to her and that is "True Friendship." I ask young people to learn to be our future encouragers to others less confidant and who have low self-esteem about themselves as well as having the gratitude from receiving an encouraging word.

Part 23: A Friend's Positive Word of Advice
Someone who has a positive opinion about a course of action or counseling.

Today's young people in America need a positive word of advice and their friends can be the perfect people to give it to them. Just the atmosphere of positivity in itself is enough to draw Erin to be receptive and eager to receive it. Erin would rather accept the positive word of advice which may be the form of counseling from Tiandre instead of seeking advice from a certified counselor. There are many reasons for his and one especially is, the fact that a certified counselor in a specialized field does not really know Erin enough to make a valid assessment regarding him, whereas Tiandre's advice will go a long ways because he knows Erin more personally.

The time spent knowing Erin is valuable indeed and gives an advantage when it comes to Tiandre listening to Erin because it is as if Tiandre can put himself in his shoes, and Tiandre can relate to Erin. A true and close friend such as Tiandre will not go out of his way to do Erin wrong or inflict harm on Erin's personality. Expecting positive words of advice from Tiandre should be the normal. Tiandre's word of advice positively attributes will go even farther if he applies the contents of his words in his own life and Erin can see Tiandre's example put into action. Tiandre will continue to advise Erin, knowing those he associates with out of school are not healthy for Erin and will bring him down if Erin does not separate from them. This positive word of advice can be more helpful if Tiandre leads by example and demonstrates how Erin's associate's negative activities are disgraceful within the community and elsewhere. Young people must be good friends and treat themselves first with dignity and respect, then giving it to other friends will be easy. Young people have the keys to success and a positive word of advice will empower them to climb the ladder of success and carry another friend.

Part 24: When a Friend's Word Counts the Most
When I am down and out, I need a friend to cheer me up.

Young people go through a host of friends who give important words which give merit of their lives. The main thing is differentiating a less powerful word from a more powerful word. Myisha's word counts the most it pertains to Tonya's health, education, career and lifestyle. All Myisha can do is give a valuable word to Tonya which carries weight then hope and pray she receives it and puts it into action. Words that count the most go beyond the phase of going in one ear and out the other. it must stick to the heart and pierce Tonya's body like never before so she feels the magnitude of this words significance.

Another important area where Myisha's words count heavily is when she puts in a good word for Tonya which helps in terns of getting a job, clearance for shortcomings, or freeing Tonya from the mockery of others. Giving Tonya a word which counts the most can open many doors and rooms of opportunities for Tonya's life. The main point for Myisha is to put her words to the best use to benefit Tonya. Tonya should be able to put all her weight on Myisha and be carried for the full ride under the wings of Myisha. Also Myisha must accept her role to give a word which will change or make a difference in Tonya's life.

Too many young people do not believe their words carry weight so a lot of times they step aside to let adults give that piece of advice, but a young life is too precious to wait on others to save them. Due to the onset of temptations and setbacks that are too unbearable at times to endure, just that immediate help can be useful at midnight when no one else is around a or cares could prove to be invaluable to help or save a young person's life. Choose to be like Myisha whose words count the most, not for recognition or notoriety for her but to help a friend to better position them for success so in turn they can help someone who needs it.

Chapter 5

What are the Gifts of Having a Friend?

Part 25: A Friend who Exhibits Love and Happiness
Someone with strong affection for another based on display of joy.

This is a topic which all young people must strive to achieve in any friendship. If you are instrumental and meaningful in your growth as a person, it will be insurmountable to your success. The benefits of friend's engaging in a strong level of love and happiness for each other will be the 'cause for many blessings now and in the future. A lot can be accomplished with friends willing to put forth the effort to have happiness, peace, and joy together for the strength of each of these elements will block out pain, suffering, and heartache. Just to have Brandon who exhibits positive traits like love and happiness is enough to help Trevor gets in a better mood regarding his position. Many times when friends want to reach their goals and dreams, it helps to have a friend to say that they care for you and no matter what or how awful you may feel and that their love is unconditional. It also helps to have Brandon who is always in a happy mood so that Trevor can begin to produce the fruits of happiness.

I love to see Brandon and Trevor wanting to share love and happiness for each other instead of trying to hurt one another. Young people are a precious commodity in our society which needs positive role models that give strong impacts and are the one who pave the way for the next generation. Depending on various circumstances, the parents of Trevor may have a hard time getting through to him which they recognize needs to change, but Brandon may be able to provide the necessary tools to help. A lot of times young people in society must do an inventory of themselves before they can act on their desire to reach to someone else, to demonstrate love and happiness because this subject is very sentimental and delicate. If this subject is not handled with the proper care then many young lives will be wasted, and this is what our society must try to avoid. So follow the example of Brandon and make sure your motives are sincere and humble when you deicide to express love and

happiness to any friend you wish to receive this.

Part 26: A Friend who Demonstrates Giving and Sharing
Those who kind do it naturally.

This topic is an important tool that should be practiced among friends who are willing to establish "True Friendship." To start off with, I believe it takes a special and unique individual to want to sacrifice something precious, Richard is aware of the law of reaping and sowing which clearly states, "What you give or share whether small or big you will receive double or plentiful. Those friends who enjoy these methods are the ones who practice this without asking any union to see Richard and Bobby sincerely enjoy the concept of giving and sharing. Richard who gives initiates the circle of prosperity, for he realizes Bobby is in need and Richard has been blessed to be able to provide for Bobby. Once Richard shares something, he creates the atmosphere of a sum of something belonging to Bobby as well and he wants him to be a part of this.

The only thing young people do not wish for, but they must stay away from is for the giver and sharer to be taken advantage of because many young people have various agendas on their minds that cause friction.

E.W.M. ENTERPRISE INC. PRESENTS…..

This topic only works for Richard and Bobby who diligently practice its good fruit. Once young people effectively practice these tools then when they grow into adulthood many goals can be achieved and many young people will not have a lacking for anything. The reason our society is in dire need of assistance with regard to basic needs is because young people do not genuinely practice these valuable traits of giving and sharing adequately with those which are in need. Richard is looked up to on the delicate topic of giving and sharing, because he knows this makes or society a better place to live when Richard and Bobby can radiate this beautiful thing. The one great thing about this topic is it rids poisonous attitudes like pride, jealously and negativity which can't snowball the effect positivity, giving and sharing provides.

Part 27: A Friend who Exhibits Caring and Assistance
Someone attentive to detail and aiding the causing by approving something.

When our youth demonstrates concern and are willing to help another person better their position, in society it is easy to see that these kids really want to establish a "True Friendship." This can be established once Tommy and Ryan show they will not allow either one to fail, sink or go down the wrong path. Tommy knows Ryan can be vulnerable to attacks from negative people and their habits, but due to Tommy's example as a concerned and helpful person he will try to prevent harm being done to Ryan. Tommy and Ryan will want to better each others status because down the road the weaker friend Ryan may need to lean on the shoulders of the stronger friend Tommy. Strong and powerful organizations like YMCA, Boy Scouts, Boys and Girls Club, and Big Brother provide activities for exercising teamwork and unity but most of all caring and assistance are exceptional tools which are exercised as well, but a lot of times they are put on the backburner. By our youth using these organizations to help Tommy will try to create a strong atmosphere for

Ryan when he cannot stand under duress of the negative tactics he might be facing and it does not necessarily have to be in a monetary sense. Our society looks at role models like young kids who perform services, young entrepreneurs, and hospital employees as being wonderful and powerful examples for our future generations.

Part 28: A Friend Who Shows Understanding
Someone having good sense and discernment; as well as mutual infinity.

This topic is a subject in terms of reaching young people who do not have much success in working out differences in their friendships with understanding. Anytime understanding is reached among two or more parties such as David and Anthony this is a powerful thing because young kids should show concern for one another on common grounds and learn to stay away from harmful issues. David understands the sorrow and pity that Anthony is going through and is willing to try to make a soothing outcome for Anthony. When young people can learn to operate on one accord and correspond efficiently with each other alliances then strength and unity can be accumulated.

Our society will always need a friend such as David who is compassionate to our needs because there are cold and mean-spirited people in our society who don't care about the next person. There are many benefits to David and Anthony working in sequence with each other to bring about understanding which many issues people engage in is not healthy. Well-being is subjects that few selected people strive for due to distraction from negative elements. Understanding must be met so when misunderstandings do happen, they can be fixed or resolved before anything gets out of hand. David and Anthony can build a strong fortress between each other when they work on the same page in regards to understanding. Once David and Anthony arrive at a sincere understanding they can do big things together which a setback or hurdle will have little to no effect on them.

Part 29: A Friend Who Exhibit's Encouragement
Someone who presents no false appearance and inspires with hope and courage.

These valuable tools of encouragement are an important part of "True Friendship" because honesty and upliftment of one another are building blocks for an enduring friendship. Zach forbids Johnny whenever he comes around him with false intentions knowing Johnny is not honest with him. Preferably, Zach should choose not to have anything to do with Johnny whenever he acts in this dishonest way. Zach is aware that before he decides to exercise encouragement for Johnny, he must be sincere in his thoughts and actions to have the best interest for Johnny. Zach wants to show that it's possible to eliminate broken relationships in our society which need mending and reconciliation.

Our youth are a joy and inspiration to be around and work with in regards to each other and adults as well. Many times our elders are removed from job positions requiring a new direction which could begin a youth movement. Zach with strong credentials who is ready to move into this position must exercise sincerity in his conduct because everybody around him will be affected. Zach must have encouraging skills because people need motivation. Zach and Johnny can be the spark for each other even as they get older because they still need innovation and ingenuity when society is composed of new technologies and equipment. The traits of encouragement are rare among friends and people in general. When you have a friend such as Zach, by all means learn to cherish him and be thankful, because he is special to Johnny's parents, classmates, workmates, and any positive human being that enjoys what Johnny has to offer

Part 30: A Friend who Exercises Integrity and Dignity
Someone exercising qualities of esteem as well as firm adherence to a standard.

This subject for our young people regarding integrity and dignity is precious in that a part of their souls and hearts can be stripped from their adversaries if they do not fight for this. Kelly and Lauren who stand firmly in this area will be well-respected amongst their peers, family members, associates, and societal members. In other words, a friend such as Kelly is not going to lower her expectations nor is she going to allow anyone to defame Lauren's character and make a mockery of Lauren. Kelly and Lauren must guard these valuable traits which gives them solidarity and completeness in their friendship. It is common for many young individual to try to break up a good thing and to attack the area of dignity and integrity is a very sensitive spot which can cause friction and in the end destroy young lives.

The reason Kelly puts up a wall of protection around this and gives an excellent example of Lauren is so Kelly can build, restore, or reconciliation any differences that they happen to be confronted with.

Many communities that need strong young leaders welcome the honorary practice of integrity and dignity demonstrated by Kelly. These traits teach discipline and show our youth how important our friendships are when they defend these qualities which will help them in any though situation. Young people must be strong when an individual will try to discourage them by letting them feel they are worthless. Once they learn to walk and talk with confidence wherever they go in life, this negative message will hardly affect them. Being aggressive is a viable tool that Kelly uses as an example to teach Laruen dignity and integrity. If Kelly were to act positive in a tough situation then this could not be helpful. Remember, anybody that does not have our best interest at heart will try to attack your weak points hoping you cannot stand on your own to fight your own battles. Do not give the adversary a foothold but walk and stand tall like a warrior who can look fear in its own eyes and let your dignity and integrity resonate strongly within you and watch the amazing results you will receive in life regarding your dreams and goals.

Chapter 6

"When you can detect whether your Friends are good or bad for you."

Part 31: The Effects of Being Judge by Your Friends
Everyone judged me but I never judge them.

This topic is very important for the youth of America, "Direction in our lives has a lot to do with our friends." You can become a big influential factor in the life of your friends. It would be important for Jessica to select and hang around good friends whether at work, school, or play to help her make quality decisions so she can avoid the pitfalls down to the road later on in life. It is important that Jessica, when in the company of her friends to conduct herself in a cordial manner, because Jessica's friends will judge her in society. Even though people have a tendency to tell their friends to judge themselves or take the speck out of your own eyes first, their friends will cast judgment to throw any stigma off them.

The effect of being judged by your friends can be immense to Jessica depending on how sensitive she is in certain areas.

Example 1: Kimberly does not have a listening ear to what is best for her, therefore the effects of good advice will not benefit Kimberly. It can only benefit those which are able to receive it and are willing to put it to use. Jessica can help Kimberly to grow and mature in certain areas which will pay big dividends in the future. Kimberly who is a trusted friend has unselfish and positive ways about her and should have confidence and faith in Jessica's judgment. Jessica is aware that alot negativity is being displayed in the society we live in these days, but she cares enough for her friend Kimberly whereas she does not want Kimberly to get discouraged with people who would cast false judgments to try to discredit her and elevate themselves. There is a sort of freedom which comes with Jessica who has only good things to say and do for Kimberly. Many mistakes and negative things can be avoided with the help of good friends showing the right path for their friend if a friend shows a listen ear.

Part 32: Do a Friend Need Their Peers Approval Concerning Societal Matters
Someone having a favorable regard of commendation or something.

There is a strong message sent out to you how you should be reaching out to help your friends concerning societal matters. Many things in our society are beneficial for you, which can mold and shape you into being a productive asset to society. Well-rounded activities such as sports, education, and job corps will allow you to be of service to others and bring out the best in your life all it take is direction and substance. There are bad habits in our society, which are dangerous to our growth. Robert needs positive words and approval from Steven who know his strengths and weakness as well as a positive peer member. If Robert were to refuse the positive approval from Steven then he would be considered a stubborn and abrasive person with no respect for what is good for him.

For example #1: Society will put in face how using drugs and alcohol can be hazardous to your life, but Steven bases his example by conducting himself in a sober fashion. When Steven warns Robert to stay away from something, which is detrimental to his growth, then Robert if exercising wisdom would do best to heed the wise advice. Steven could be a lifesaver in terms of the wrong road Robert many decided to take. Many people in society with degrees and certification from schools around the world believe their advice or approval of a matter can be powerful enough to change your life for the better, but a close and trustworthy friend such as Steven can better give necessary approval for Robert who may need it in a crucial period. By being a curious and experimental type person in activities you engage in can hurt yourself if you have not done your homework or research regarding these activities.

Robert must put aside his pride giving earnest attentiveness to the positive approval of Steven who wants to see him do well. One day Steven with the same goals as Robert might need some valuable help in an area which Robert may be of assistance. It is safe to say most societal matters such as health, business, and education are necessary and a positive person approval does wonders.

Part 33: The Importance of Working Together in Being Part of the Solution
Someone involved in solving a problem, avoiding controversy as a hindrance.

I really enjoy speaking to the hearts of youth who have experienced a peer member being part of a solution to a matter taking precedence over disagreement between friends. It is easy to say debates and differences of opinions are common among yourself these days, but to exercise enough sense to be apart of a solution should not be a tough task for you to follow. Nathan does not want to dwell in the arena of problems all his life, but Nathan must find better ways to answer problems giving hope to Oscar and be willing to try them himself. It is hard to accept Oscar on a team consisting of solution-makers because of the differences he has with Nathan but possibilities are foreseeable if their priorities are in order.

For example #1: Anytime there is a matter between Oscar and Nathan which requires a solution and two heads put together are better than one. It is important to create an atmosphere where Oscar and Nathan can expand their horizons utilizing their innovative skills and unique personalities to bring fresh ideas to the plate. You can play an integral role in the new technology and advancing methods which our society is hungry and in need to have. True enough, iron sharpens iron and Nathan's peer members could be vital to the mastery of a project which is in need of Oscar's assistance to get off the ground. It would be trivial to prohibit Nathan admirable assistance in the making of an astounding project only to give weight to less related matters. You must realize when you are upset or angry, "You will get over it," while you have so many things in common especially, with your peer members who have high goals they challenge each other to put their differences behind them as well. So the possibility is high in that Oscar and Nathan can join in a partnership to be the part of a solution which helps to advance a cause or better something for a greater value.

Part 34: A Friend that Make a Difference in Your Life to Becoming a Positive Influence
Someone with the power to intangibly affect a person or event.

This is a subject which helps who needs to eradicate bad seeds, meaning bad-influences from your life and fill this void with good influences. Society will try to block you by saying that a tall order is before you when it comes to the changing of something. Joseph has the tools and equipment within himself, if utilized effectively to be the vehicle to bring about a dramatic change in Hectors life who exhibits bad influences whomever he meets. When Joseph sees Hector, deviating from the right path Joseph will surround Hector with an influx of positive peer members to engage in positive activities on a daily basis to help Hector see his need for change. Remember change requires effort and to stay as you are is easy to do especially if you are not willing to better yourself.

Example #1: Joseph recognizes the benefits of being a positive influence to others around him because they can make a difference in other people's lives for the better. Joseph does not want Hector, the bad influence peer to rot in bitterness and negativity, for Joseph cares about Hector for his own well-being. Joseph knows a lot of our hindrances come from bad influences getting us off on the wrong foot. Joseph knows how meaningful it is for Hector who has a desire to do good and wants positive people around him to help shape Hector into a well-rounded individual, so Joseph is going to do everything in his power to see that Hector is given this. First and foremost, to bring a change in Hector life requires effort, determination, and willingness to help him who's going down the road of destruction. These individuals are rare and few such as Joseph who will sacrifice anything to see Hector make something of his life. You can be left to make difficult decisions which require help from a caring individual who hates to see bad traits exemplified in you and sees the positive values and influences brought into fruition in your life.

Part 35: The Valuable Lessons Friends can Learn Through Mutual Understanding in the Issues they Face Daily
Communication brings understanding.

This is a topic friends can come to terms on an agreement having positive results. Mutual understanding can be achieved between Greg and Joe who could care less about being greedy, selfish, or prideful when both coincide with each other to reach the same goal. Greg wants what is best for Joe just as much as Joe wants what is best for Greg. I am pretty sure many societal issues concerning elements which are harmful and negative like drugs, illicit material communicated through television and radio negative groups and associations which are not healthy are issues which Greg and Joe are willing to address to try to rectify. The main thing between the two is that a mutual understanding can be obtained regardless of the topic being addressed as long as both sides are on the same page regarding the outcome.

Example #1: If Greg pursues trying to solve a solution to a societal matter with someone who is negative, then no mutual understanding can ever be brought about which is a valuable lesson for you to learn and benefit from. The choice and selection falls in the hands of Greg who must be wise and prudent to engage with Joe who will create an atmosphere for mutual understand to occur. Sure the possibilities are high but the degree of a favorable results fall within you and a good friend involved. You can possess so much energy at a young age to the point hat you can make decisions without exercising patience and candor. Anytime Joe operates in ignorance and stupidity he should not be mocked first of all and secondly, Joe should be told with care and concern how his impropriety is unacceptable. Greg who has the mindset for "True Friendship" will be guided by a strong desire to fight illiteracy, unethical practices, and insubordinate behavior which Joe may be exercising. Greg has a host of experience in the area of mutual understanding recognizing value it holds in a "True Friendship" in helping Joe. Joe knows that Greg wants what is best for him and if a valuable lesson is being taught in them working together then he is supportive of this.

Part 36: The Ways a Friend can Work with a Devils-Advocate to Keep from Creating Animosity
Someone who is an adverse critic, especially of a good cause.

This topic comes in a time when the role as a devils-advocate peer member plays can be helpful in the long run. Regardless of the role Nikki plays it is needful even to Yvette because she does not like someone who always agrees being, "A Yes Man to everything." Society comes to believe that some of our youth do not possess the backbone to stand up for themselves. These young people, although they may have good intentions will lose a lot of respect amongst their peer members and associates.

Example #1: Yvette must keep a positive vibe around Nikki, because even though Nikki may disagree with Yvette on several subjects, the overall goal they engage in is a good cause. This means Yvette does not want to stir up hostility or let Nikki know animosity will be the end result. So Nikki and Yvette should try to keep things at bay being that neither one of them will look for the worst in the matter. Yvette main teaching tool to Nikki is to look at the bigger picture being open and receptive to a wide variety of ideals which both of them may overlook that could be the missing piece to a puzzle. The bottom line lessons are learned and self-growth are developed when you expand your thought processes believing all things are possible to those that believe. Nikki who may never fit the criteria of perfection and pleasing to Yvette as a devil-advocate peer member still can be helped to see areas where she needs more maturity and Yvette can give Nikki the right tools to achieve this.

Example #2: The good thing about this is that Yvette is a strong-willed individual who will not allow negativity to seep in nor will she let animosity have a foothold on the outcome with a matter concerning Nikki. It is important that you work towards harmonious solutions in given subjects along with your respect for each others opinions not trying to allow strife to set precedence on issues that are brought up.

Chapter 7

"The Positive Opportunities behind Being a Friend"

Part 37: A Friend who Receives Promotions and Second Chances
Someone who thrives on the advancement in rank and greater chances.

I really like speaking on the subject of promotions and second chances because you deserve it when most people do not want to give you another opportunity. Cassandra relishing in an advancement or rank from her status will want to surround herself along with Jeffrey in keeping positivity in their arena. Cassandra receiving these promotions and second chances must be humble and grateful or this and with good on others who have the opportunity to receive promotions and second changes. Jeffrey should not give up or quit when there is a window of opportunity still left to achieve a goal. Sometimes when promotions are granted to you people in society do not appreciate them because they operate in envy towards you who worked hard to achieve this. Cassandra can cherish the reign of second chances with Jeffery and not have to be too concerned about animosity. When you strive for "True Friendship," good things will happen for you that come with the territory of opportunities.

Example #1: Cassandra and Jeffery who care for one another want to see each other progress whether in school, work, or play. The main thing for Jeffery to do is to never give up when he comes short of reach his goal. Through second chances, Jeffery can choose an alternative route to get him where he wants to be. Cassandra know that taking advantage of her promotions and second chance can never be expressed enough, so it is important that she go all out to make a good showing. In addition, Cassandra is willing to prove to Jeffery how far he can climb the ladder of success so she can convince Jeffery and others she is not taking this opportunity for granted. You may not be use to receiving a denial rejection when a supervisor at a job or a teacher does not pick you for a better position so you are quick to play the blame game. Cassandra recognizes that Jeffrey must work hard, stay positive, and wish other people the best so when he is presented a chance to do promotional work and given the opportunity to be a role model he will not be surprised.

Part 38: A Friend Who Reaches a Goal with the Help of His Community

Someone who accomplishes something through the assistance of others.

You need support to ensure the right type of guidance necessary for your development and growth. Michael probably does not have the tools within himself, family members, or classmates to propel Walter beyond reaching his goals. The support and backbone of various positive community groups may be the answer to Walter's success. Local groups within the communities such as the YMCA, Boys and Girls Clubs, and Boy Scouts are few examples, which Walter can enroll into and meet the goals he is striving to achieve. Usually Walter would not have to wait on sighing up for these positive groups within his community, but if he do and desires to change Walter can do this with Michael whom has a big vision for success which are encouraging for our youth needing it.

Example #1: Communities hold block meetings for the specific purpose of eradicating the negativity, which occur in their respective regions to get together to try to arrive at solutions to their concerns along with coming up with tools to shape and mold you into becoming the future powerful leader our society needs. Another valuable option Walter may seek within the community is the consultation of pillars and notable activists whom may make an impact on helping Walter reach his goals. Such individuals are fighters for a good cause and through their role as servants within the community; they want to make sure that Walter's potential is fully materialized. When your success rate is being exhibited in terms of employment, education, and business this becomes a positive sign in preserving your life instead of incarceration in confinement centers, innocent young lives being victimized by crime, and the dropout rate in schools. Walter should aspire to do something great with his life and to boldly seek the help of community advisors to become instrumental in his success. Most programs initiated for Walter to participate in by a community set dormant because he needs to be enthusiastically motivated to get himself going. It is always good for you to remember to advertise doors that are always open to those willing to reach out to you and to the youth who may seek to receive this help.

Part 39: A Friend Who Partakes of Favorable Circumstances Regarding her Close Friend

Someone who joins in something advantageous concerning a friend.

You should want to be a part of anything involving success concerning your close friend. A good indication of this is when Trisha is excelling in school, work, or a project which shows immense growth in her development which Dominique sees and desires the opportunity for her to grow as well. Just to be a part of a successful endeavor can mount a motivating factor for Trisha's aspirations and goals. When Trisha and Dominique learn to work together in achieving a common goal putting aside trivial ideals and staying focus on the bigger picture, than anything is possible for them. Dominique is willing to defend or protect Trisha from anything detrimental to her success. Many times you can be eager to pursue favorable circumstance not knowing opposition from adversary comes with the territory. So in the event of this occurring you should always try to employ a trustworthy friend who will do what it takes to prevent something catastrophe form happening.

Example #1: When the doors of opportunity open for Trisha to climb the ladder of success, it would be wise to make careful decisions throughout this process and to seek the assistance of Dominique. Dominique knows that reaching out to help Trisha whom she has her best interest at heart will generate success in her own business. You can play an integral part in the fabric of the new ideas, advancement, and technologies our society has to offer. Always keep an open mind when the doors of opportunities are presented to you and get involved and find out where you can be of help to a much needed friend or cause.

Part 40: The Friend who Values Keeping a Promise
All I got is my word.

You will be reckoned with the highest esteem when you learn to keep promises. A broken promise will show that your character has flaws and nobody wants to be around you and let alone have anything to do with you. Many broken homes, tarnished relationships and negative scenes are derived from broken promises which occur every day in our society. The future is bright and blossoming for Byisha who puts big emphasis on what is guaranteed. Even though Byisha may take lightly Ana who is close to her, she will not break her promise, it can occur, and therefore Byisha must bring it to Ana's attention that our friendship is too valuable for us not to keep our promises solid.

Example #1: Byisha who walks with her head held high when made a promise and has no weakness can go anywhere being respected and admired for her sincerity in keeping her vow. When Byisha keeps her promise to Ana about something, Byisha has strong sense of responsibility towards Ana to know how much Ana can count on her to come through. Society says "Records are meant to be broken," but in regards to promises being made you can hurt people close to you who have high expectations for you. The best thing to do is to not make a promise at all that you cannot keep. When Byisha practices consistently in keeping her promises to Ana her close friend and other associates, they have no problem recommending her to successful people who like to be around a friend such as Byisha and enjoy her company. There are times when you can promise to never hurt someone again or not let them down. Which you can make that has nothing to do with being broken promises or not. You will have a strong and healthy friendship with your family members, schoolmates, and playmates with no strife when you learn to practice keeping your promises and having harmony will always be present.

Part 41: A Friend who sees the Importance of Motivating You to Success
Someone who provides an incentive in reaching a goal in being successful.

You should always have the aspirations to want to be successful in your endeavors in whatever field of interest you choose in life. The only thing of concern is our society needs people such as yourself who willing to fulfill their goals despite the odds that may be against you to not succeed. You must make sure that at least the lack of motivation was not the reason for you not succeeding in your goals. Role models, mentors and parents who emphasize a solid foundation for their children do play a big roel and have a big impact in the decisions a motivated individual makes. Now, our society is in dire need of more scientist, entrepreneurs, specialist in research fields and potentially motivated people such as yourself who can be the true shapers and molders of our future making a difference.

Example #1: Shantay believes that her motivation is what is necessary to propel her to be successful in the competitive society we live in. She tries to lead by example for Nita in letting her know that drive and determination behind what you plan is a powerful trait to possess. Nita has experienced situations where fatigue or the brink of giving up had set in, but by being motivated, this was enough to carry her through to be successful. Another important thing Shantay wants Nita to be aware of is that just her talents and gift alone may not be enough for her to be victorious in whatever endeavors she might be pursuing especially with the absence of motivation. You can be an average non-skilled individual but with strong motivation and hustle behind your efforts, you are a force to be reckoned with. Shantay mentioned to Nita that just because she many an underdog going into an event Nita still possess a chance of being successful if she earnestly rely on her motivation. Remember, it is not the beginning of a situation that counts but the finishing part that carries the most weight and to exhibit motivation will put fear in your opponent when she knows she has her work cut out for her.

Chapter 8

"The Friend who sees the Value in Cultivating our Potential"

Part 42: The Friend who does not allow his friend to waste his talent
Someone who will not allow a talent to depreciate and go down the tube.

I really enjoy introducing this subject to you knowing that you have your friend's back and want him to fulfill his goals and not waste his talents. Edward recognizes that it takes a great deal of humility and sacrifice to help Reuben develop his abilities and talents to the fullest, not allowing them to be wasted. If Edward is willing to put aside his selfish agenda and help Reuben to bring his talent to fruition, he is a special and wonderful person indeed. Edward needs to take into consideration the competition, which exists in society and especially how Reuben could be adamant and getting, caught up in it. If Edward knows Reuben can use the proper tools and equipment surrounding him, he can achieve his goals. Then it is only common sense for Edward to help him or refer Reuben to the help he needs to be successful.

Example #1: Edward plays an integral role in Reuben's life if he truly cares and wants the best for him. Edward bears witnesses to Reuben's are talent, which he exhibits, to Edward and his classmates at school in his art class. Edward is stern on his friend Reuben and encourages him to spend quality time in his art project and be creative in many art careers, such as a cartoonist, doing community art projects, and purse strongly his own art business which can elevate Reuben's talent and not have him become a dormant. Edward knows that Reuben is gifted but does not want to lose interest in his talent and altogether let it go to waste.

Example #2: Another example of mentorship is my good friend Kevin who brought out the writing talents of me, who did not have the zeal or enthusiasm at first to write, but being motivated to see the therapeutic benefits of writing as being an art expressing everyday subjects in which we all encounter and giving our audience a better understanding by putting them right there at the scene walking them through it has been a wonderful experience.

Part 43: A Friend who knows the Importance of being Goal-Oriented
Someone who values the objective towards which an endeavor is directed.

You will break through many barriers and climb through many hurdles, which come your way if you are in the area of being goal-oriented. Willie knows the good thing about being goal-oriented is that he knows what he is striving for with a purpose involved, how long it will take to get there, and the tools and equipment he will need to get the job done. Willie encourages Raymond to keep his eyes on the prize despite storms. Raymond may go through things which may try to discourage him. Willie is aware of the value of being driven and the stick-it-to-tive-ness that is necessary in seeing his goals achieve because no matter what happens he will never look back until he is successful. Raymond especially loves to be around Willie specifically because of this special trait that Willie possess.

Example #1: Willie recognizes the balance it gives Raymond life once he decides to become goal-oriented in terms of structure and the short-term goals are just as important as the long-terms goals Raymond set for himself. You can best believe a friend whom you care for deeply as well as yourself will be far ahead of your peers when you set goals for yourself as oppose to someone who just go about his life with no purpose or direction. You can pave the way for a beautiful start for the next generation and this gives our society strength to have you utilizing your potential along with realistic goals being set making a difference in your community. May you become the first one to be the heart and soul of your community giving it an identity instead of being a statistic to our confinement centers and running the streets with no purpose and not being useful in life? Willie knows that taking risk in life as well as putting up the best shot he has to offer as far as setting goals, which are unique to the common individual, comes with the territory but being industrious and bold in his approach will only pay big dividends for him in the future. Set your goals to the point whereas it is as close as tasting the thrill of victory and you will not be denied.

Part 44: A Friend who is a Possibility Thinker
You have to be a thinker stay in the game.

You need to visualize yourself in a prosperous society breaking barriers of hopelessness and impossibilities by becoming possibility thinker. To be honest before an undertaking of any project being a success, you must first conceive the thought of it ever happening. If, Carlos is always thinking positive thoughts, then the threshold of him achieving his goals and being brought into fruition. Carlos is someone who is looking to help Marquees who lacks confidence and self-esteem whose word does not carry merit. Carlos is aware of the chances of favorable development, which are in the realm of possibility or happening without contradiction proven facts, laws, or circumstance. Carlos is trying to let Marquees, now that basically, it is like saying, "In the meantime purse your objective until you have achieved your goal; you hold the keys to the power behind your belief that something can be brought into fruition.

Example #1: Marquees who is sometimes negative in his thinking and personality will do best to surround himself with Carlos and other friends who are possibility thinkers to help him out of his dilemmas. Carlos has the qualities of a possibility thinker who will not limit or put boundaries on himself because he firmly believes he will prevail against all odds. In addition, Carlos knows Marquees can become a powerful motivation speaker helping his peers and associates gain direction. Now, Marquees who once before entertained negative and destructive thoughts can face his challenges and storms when exhibiting possibility thinking which helps Marquees enormously towards overcoming his hurdles. Carlos is a rare gem to find and solidifies the goal in term of what "True Friendship" is about.

Part 45: A Friend who enjoys Go-Getters
Real networkers 100%

You can fit the criteria of a "Go-Getter" in bringing inspiration and ambition to the table for yourself and friends who need this quality to get them going. Go-getters are people who make things happen, but need to be led to use their creative power in a positive way. Joshua is diligent going after what he wants in life not waiting on Christopher or others to do it for him. Joshua thrives on surrounding himself around Christopher because the determination to be successful is there and he can absorb its fruits. Another beautiful trait of Joshua is how he produces energy towards the objected of a goal instead of being lazy and idle which is a wasted in itself.

Example #1: Joshua sets a trend for Christopher when it comes to wanting something out of life. You will always have friends who are discouraged and lack faith in themselves so you being a go-getter exemplifying this positive trait can be the one to break them out of this shell. Joshua is one whom Christopher would want for Joshua to introduce himself to Christopher's parents, teacher, or co-employers because he is an enlighten role model. You need positive influences in helping you direct your path that are big impacts to your growth and development. You do not see many people aspiring to be go-getters these days because it requires effort, drive, and motivation to consistently push yourself to the limit. Go-getters rub off on people beautifully with the intensity and adrenaline they possess behind their energetic nature and you will do well to corral yourself around these people. Joshua and Christopher are remarkable examples of the value in becoming a go-getter to you and you do wise to follow them. It is considered a treat when you exercise go-getter qualities around your friends.

Part 46: A Friend who is a Positive Force in a Competitive World
Someone who is positive with the test of skills, abilities and spreading it.

You will notice that it takes a great deal of humility to take a step back when engaging in events requiring competition along with being positive at the same time. You can hunger to win so bad but try to keep fairness in its place when competing with your friends because this is a positive trait. Breonya is aware that teamwork, good ethical behavior, and a good spirit are important to carry with her wherever she goes in society to be successful. Breonya does not believe in competing with Keonya for the wrong reasons flowing on her competitive juices as long as positivity is present then it's a win-win situation.

Example #1: Breonya relishes the role our society needs when it comes to looking for champions in competitive events. Breonya wants to show Keonya that a positive force can be demonstrated in our competitive society without holding personal vendettas against each other. Many adults who look for the potential that you possess want you to exhibit good character showing that can be trusted with our future, because remember the youth is our future. Breonya knows that possessing positive qualities can easily draw friends around her but she just wants to give Keonya and others a positive influence in which to follow. Breonya is a rock to Keonya when Breonya demonstrates this quality whether going out to the movies together, the recreational center, or just hanging out with family friends. Breonya understands that it is not about winning and losing but how you play the game that's what counts the most. You have to keep your sight on the big picture because competition is healthy, but should not allow you to take your focus off what is most important and that is "True Friendship."

About the Author

Eric Martin grew up in Richmond, CA.

He is CEO of EWM Enterprise INC, a company specializing in business, finance, publishing, marketing, but overall straight networking. Although he travels throughout the country, he makes time for helping the disadvantaged youth and has a series of life skills books and workshops in the works.

A loving husband and father, his life serves as a role model for his children and youth in America.

Anyone who wants to contact the Author for speeches or public appearances and/or donate funds contact by email at: ericmartin@mail.com or ewmenterpriseinc@mail.com